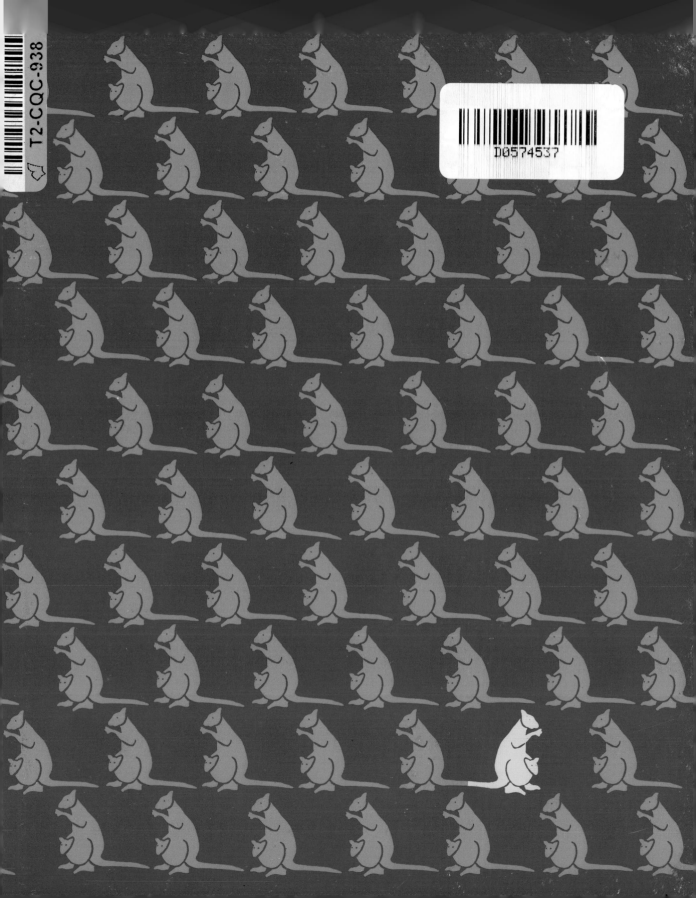

# A DORLING KINDERSLEY BOOK

Conceived, edited, and designed by DK Direct Limited

## Note to parents

**What's Inside? Baby** is designed to help young children understand the fascinating ways different babies develop. It illustrates how a child grows inside its mother, how a baby sea horse is born, and what is inside a bird's egg. It is a book for you and your child to read and talk about together, and to enjoy.

**Designers**   Sonia Whillock and Juliette Norsworthy
**Typographic Designer**   Nigel Coath
**US Editor**   B. Alison Weir
**Editor**   Sarah Phillips
**Design Director**   Ed Day
**Editorial Director**   Jonathan Reed

**Illustrator**   Richard Manning
**Cover Photograph**   Fiona Pragoff
**Photographers**   Karl Shone, Frank Greenaway, and Fiona Pragoff
**Photograph page 16**   Jane Burton/Bruce Coleman Limited
**Writer**   Alexandra Parsons

Animals supplied by Trevor Smith's Animal World

First American Edition, 1992

10 9 8 7 6 5 4 3 2

Published in the United States by
Dorling Kindersley, Inc., 95 Madison Avenue
New York, New York 10016

**Library of Congress Cataloging-in-Publication Data**
Baby. – 1st American ed.
   p.   cm. – (What's inside?)
Summary: Describes the early development, both before and after birth,
of the young of such animals as the crocodile, Shetland pony, and human being.
   ISBN 1-56458-004-0
1. Embryology – Juvenile literature.   2. Embryology – Human – Juvenile literature.
[1. Embryology.   2. Birth.   3. Animals – Infancy.]   I. Dorling Kindersley, Inc.   II. Series.
QM601.B33   1992
591.3'3 — dc20                                                      91–58213
                                                                          CIP
                                                                          AC

Printed in Italy

# WHAT'S INSIDE?

# BABY

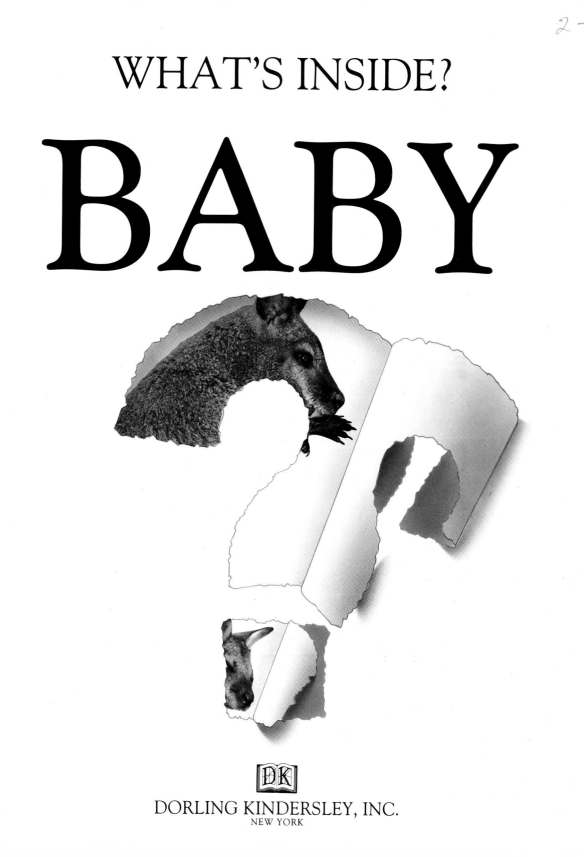

DORLING KINDERSLEY, INC.
NEW YORK

# HUMAN BEINGS

You started life as a tiny speck inside your mother's belly. As you grew inside, you discovered how to move your arms and legs, how to suck and swallow, and how to practice breathing.

While she was waiting for you to be born, your mother's breasts became full of milk for her to feed you.

As you grew, your mother's belly got bigger. It took you nine months to grow into a baby.

Your mother could feel you kicking here, inside her belly.

The womb is the warm, stretchy place inside women where babies grow.

The mother's blood takes food and oxygen to the placenta, a spongy organ inside the womb.

The baby is attached to the placenta by a special tube called the umbilical cord. Food and oxygen go through it and into the baby's body.

The growing baby floats around comfortably in a sac of water. Most babies like to rest upside down.

# DOGS

Mother dogs can have as many as eight puppies at once. The puppies are blind and deaf when they are born, but they can smell. When they are about two weeks old, they start to see and hear.

Birthing is hard work for a mother dog. She will need extra food in the days before her puppies are born.

This dog has eight teats, one for each puppy to drink milk from.

Puppies grow inside their mothers for about 60 days. This retriever will give birth in a few days.

Puppies grow stronger and learn a lot when they are playing. They grow up very quickly – a puppy can become a mother when she is only one year old!

Each puppy grows in its own water sac and has its own umbilical cord.

This is the mother's birth canal. The puppies will come out of this opening.

A dog's womb is U-shaped, with puppies growing from both sides.

# SHETLAND PONIES

The Shetland pony is one of the smallest horses in the world. Like all horses and ponies, it likes to be on the move. Its babies can get up and walk minutes after they have been born.

This is a mother horse.
She is called a mare.
Her baby is called a foal.

A foal takes a long time to grow in the womb – even longer than it takes humans. Mares are pregnant for 11 months.

The mare's belly gets bigger as the foal grows inside her.

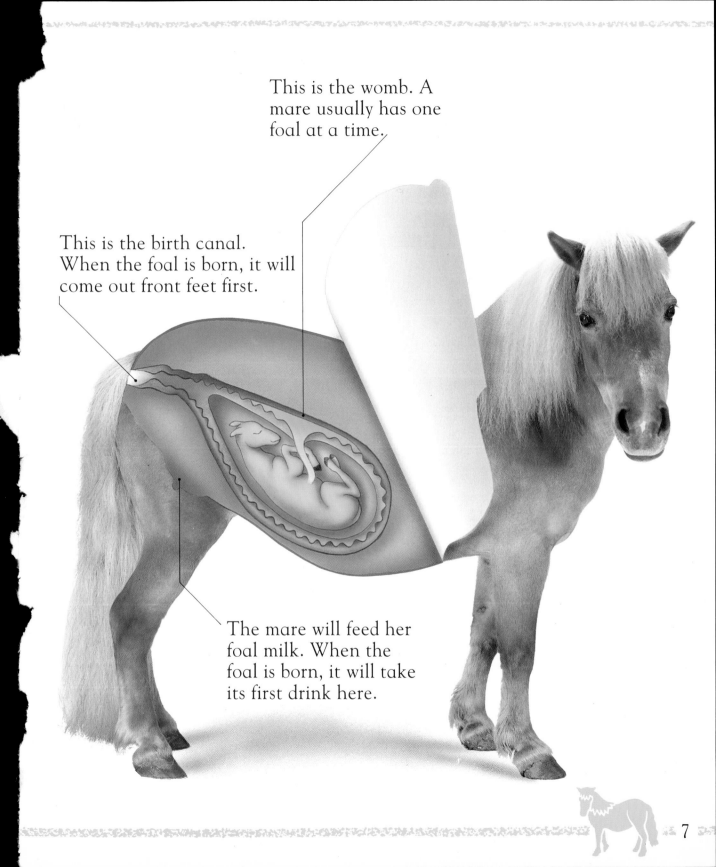

This is the womb. A mare usually has one foal at a time.

This is the birth canal. When the foal is born, it will come out front feet first.

The mare will feed her foal milk. When the foal is born, it will take its first drink here.

7

# PORCUPINES

Mother porcupines give birth to two or three babies at a time. The babies are born with soft quills. They stay in the nest until they are about two weeks old, when their quills harden.

The porcupine's coat of sharp quills protects it from enemies. _____

Baby porcupines grow for about three months inside their mothers.

Crested porcupines live in burrows under the ground. They come out at night to feed. They can't see well, but their sense of smell is very good.

Some porcupines can climb trees. They have long, strong tails and use them to hold on to branches. Long-tailed porcupines live in North and South America.

This is the mother's birth canal. Because the babies' quills are soft and silky, they don't scratch her during birth.

This porcupine has one baby in each side of her womb.

# WALLABIES

A baby wallaby does not stay long in its mother's belly. When it is born, it is blind, bald, and the size of a Boston bean. It climbs into its mother's pouch and continues growing there. Baby wallabies are called joeys.

This joey is about eight months old. It still hops back into its mother's pouch when frightened, tired, or thirsty.

This is the entrance to the pouch.

Hidden inside the pouch is this joey's little brother, who is only a few weeks old.

Wallabies have strong legs. They can run very quickly – even with a joey in the pouch.

A mother wallaby can take care of two babies, one much younger than the other. They share her pouch and she feeds them milk.

Each baby sucks from its own teat, and always comes back to the same one.

This joey's little brother is too small to suck, so milk is squirted into its mouth.

# BIRDS

A baby bird does not develop inside its mother. It grows inside an egg which is filled with food for the developing bird. The mother bird lays the egg in a nest and keeps it warm until the baby bird, or chick, is ready to hatch out of its shell.

A raven chick is growing inside this egg.

Eggs have one round end and one pointed end. The baby bird's head develops near the egg's rounded end.

Eggs are patterned with blots and splotches to hide them in their surroundings.

Most newborn chicks need a lot of care. Their parents find food for them until they are old enough to fly and hunt for themselves.

This is the yolk. The bird feeds on it as it grows.

This baby bird will take about two weeks to develop. It will be born with its eyes closed and no feathers.

As the raven grows, the shell gets thinner, so air can get inside.

# CROCODILES

Mother crocodiles lay lots of eggs in warm, sandy nests. Crocodile eggs make a tasty breakfast for many jungle animals, so the mother guards her eggs carefully.

Crocodiles are one of the oldest inhabitants of the Earth. These toothy creatures have been roaming riverbanks since the time of the dinosaurs.

Crocodiles usually lay their eggs at night. They lay about 80 eggs at once because so many of them are stolen before they hatch.

After about three months, the baby crocodile is ready to hatch. It chips its way out of its egg.

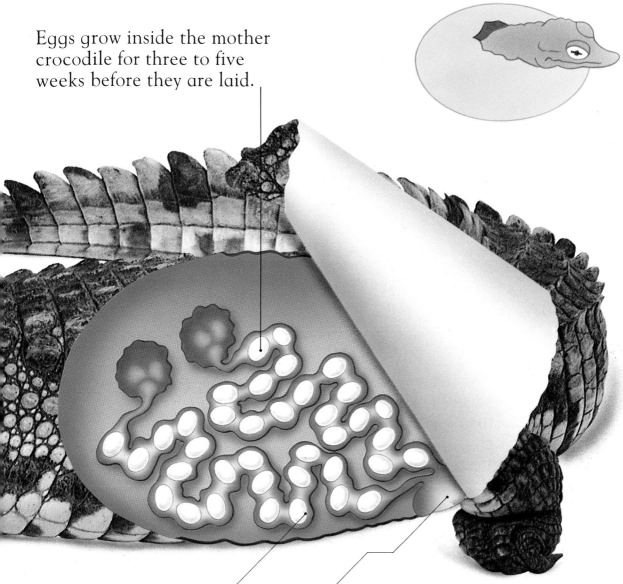

Eggs grow inside the mother crocodile for three to five weeks before they are laid.

These eggs are lined up inside the crocodile, ready to be laid.

This is where the eggs come out. Sometimes the mother lays an egg on her foot and lowers it gently into the nest.

15

# SEA HORSES

When it comes to having babies, the father sea horse does all the work. The mother lays her eggs in his special pouch and swims off. The baby sea horses grow inside their father's pouch.

The pouch is like a pocket. It can hold as many as 200 eggs.

When the babies have grown, the father wraps his long tail around a piece of seaweed to anchor himself.

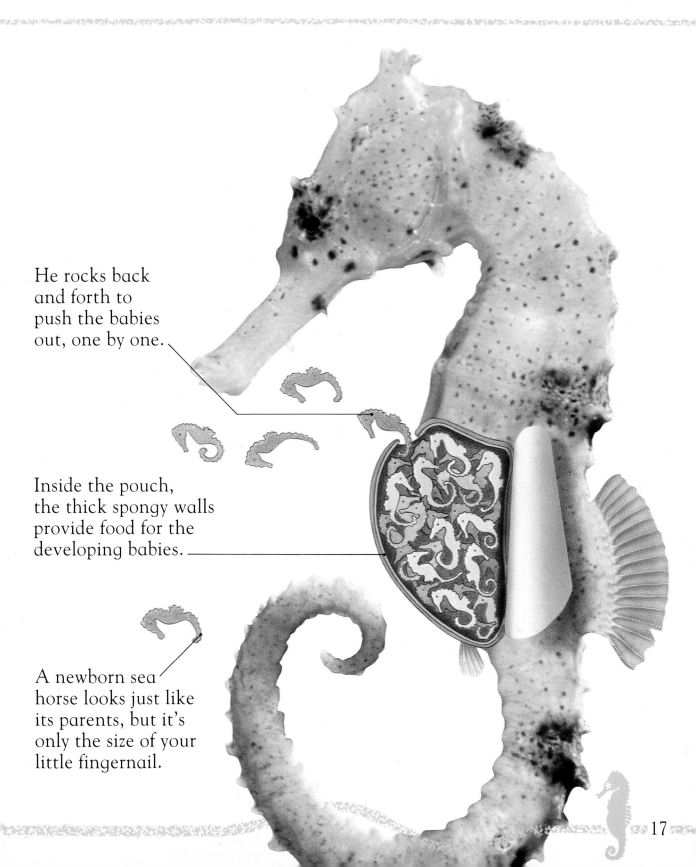

He rocks back and forth to push the babies out, one by one.

Inside the pouch, the thick spongy walls provide food for the developing babies.

A newborn sea horse looks just like its parents, but it's only the size of your little fingernail.

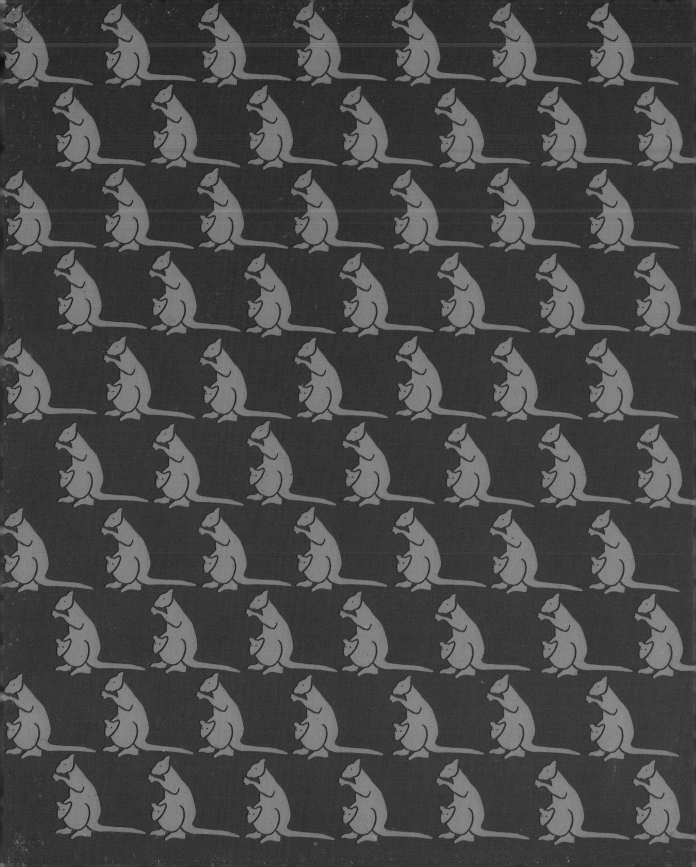